English for the Thoughtful Child

VOLUME ONE

Eighth Printing, 2003

Greenleaf Press
www.greenleafpress.com
3761 Hwy 109 North, Lebanon, TN 37087

Phone (615) 449-1617
Fax (615) 449-4018
Orders (800) 311-1508

English for the Thoughtful Child

VOLUME ONE

Mary F. Hyde
revised & edited by cynthia A. Shearer

Greenleaf Press

Lebanon, Tennessee

Contents

i

Introduction

I had a long list of things I wanted to find in a first grammar and composition text.

I wanted a text that would incorporate dictation, memorization, oral composition, and what Charlotte Mason called narration (in which a child makes a story his own by putting it into his own words). I knew from experience that these goals would get lost in the shuffle if they were not clearly laid out for me. This book is structured around those goals.

With five children (at that time) to care for, I needed a text that would be *simple* and at least pleasant to work with, both for me and my children. This book is enjoyable, and there is no need to constantly flip through a separate teacher's edition; everything I need is in one place.

I wanted my children to have good literary models, neither silly nor stuffy. This book uses selections from Aesop's fables, as well as poems by Robert Louis Stevenson, Sara Coleridge, Lucy Larcom and others.

I wanted material that would concentrate on the writing process, and yet not burden the young child; I wanted a text that would draw the child into writing. Hyde uses "picture lessons" to stimulate the child's imagination. She focuses the student's attention on a wonderful picture, and suggests questions for the teacher to use in eliciting observations and ideas, as student and teacher look at the illustration together. After the child has had time to thoroughly study the picture, the writing begins. These exercises allow for a time of "pre-writing," during which ideas are allowed to germinate before the child is required to begin actual writing. This approach lays the foundation for good composition skills that can be applied in all learning situations.

I wanted a book that would teach English in a natural context, not in artificial isolation. One of the better features of this book is the interdisciplinary nature of the exercises. For example, Lesson 46 teaches the correct usage of *have* and *has*, but children also learn about the characteristics of insects. Another lessons asks, "What signs of spring have you noticed? Which birds come first, and when do they arrive?" The text asks questions that encourage children to be good observers of their surroundings.

When I found this book, I knew I had found the book I wanted to use. It maintains a gentle, thoughtful tone, perfect for use as a first course in English. I use this book for our second grade English text, but it is also very useful as a first course for older reluctant writers. We hope you will enjoy it as well as we have.

Cyndy Shearer

To the Teacher

Adapted from the original preface to Two-Book Course in English, *by Mary F. Hyde, 1900.*

It is not expected that the exact amount of work laid out in each lesson will be all that is required for every class. Such additional exercises should be given as the needs of the class demand.

All written work must be carefully done. Whenever the pupil constructs a sentence, whether to illustrate the use of a word or to state a fact, he should be required to do the work in such a manner as to increase his power of thought and cultivate his power of expression. He should be inspired to put forth his best effort in every exercise.

There must be a constant application of the facts learned. Keep a record of the most common errors committed by pupils in their written work, and prepare simple dictation exercises containing the correct forms of the misused words or expressions.

When you are ready to give a dictation exercise, read each sentence slowly once (unless the sentence is long), then require the class to write it. In dictating a long sentence, a paragraph, a stanza of poetry, a letter, or any similar matter, first read the entire selection through, then dictate the separate parts in the same way that you would dictate a short sentence.

Much of the work, particularly in composition, is meant to be suggestive merely. All school studies afford good material for work in composition. Whatever the pupil is interested in, whether it be a topic connected with his reading, geography, history, nature, or other lessons, will furnish him a good subject for composition.

Pupils should tell and retell in their own words the fables and myths contained in the book, until they become so familiar with the stories that they can never forget them. There should also be frequent repetition of the poems that are committed to memory.

The sentences in bold type are to be used in developing the various subjects. The pupils should read these sentences from the book, and should answer orally such questions on them as may be asked. The questions in plain type are for the use of the teacher, but they should not be followed too closely. The teacher should add such questions of her own as may be needed to make the subject clear. The italic sentences are instructions.

Attention to the language used by pupils should not be confined to the recitation period in English. Every statement made, every question answered in the course of a lesson in arithmetic, geography, history, or other study, should be expressed in clear, accurate, straightforward English.

Lesson 1
THE SENTENCE

1. Tell something about your book.
2. Tell something about your pencil.
3. Tell something about your desk.
4. Think of some object at your home. Tell something about the object.
5. Think of something that you saw on your way to school. Tell what you saw.
6. Tell what you think about the weather today.
7. Ask something that you would like to know about the weather tomorrow.

When you use words to express a complete thought, you make a **sentence**.

Read these sentences.

> **The sun is shining.**
> **The sky is blue.**
> **Look at the clouds.**
> **Which way is the wind blowing?**

1. What is the first sentence about?
2. What is the second sentence about?
3. What does the third sentence do?
4. What does the fourth sentence do?

| A **sentence** is the expression of a complete thought in words. |

EXERCISE 1

Copy these sentences. Use your very best handwriting.

1. Look at this butterfly. _____

_____

2. It has bright yellow wings. _____

_____

3. The wings are striped with black. _____

_____

4. On what do butterflies live? _____

_____

EXERCISE 2

Mark the groups of words that do not express a complete thought.

> Going to church yesterday
> We will order these books
> Martha and Jack and their black spotted dog

Look at the groups you marked. How would you make them into complete sentences?
In the space below, rewrite one of the above incomplete thoughts as a complete sentence.

_____

_____

_____

Lesson 2
STATEMENTS

Autumn is here.
Crickets chirp.
The swallows have gone.

1. About what does the first sentence tell? What is told about it?
2. About what does the second sentence tell? What is told about them?
3. What does the third sentence tell?
4. Give a sentence telling something about a hat.
5. Give a sentence telling what you like to do.
6. Give a sentence that tells your age.
7. Give a sentence that tells where you live.

A sentence that tells or states something is called a statement.

---

1. With what kind of letter does the first statement in this lesson begin?
2. With what kind of letter does the second statement begin?
3. With what kind of letter does the third statement begin?
4. What mark is placed after the first statement?
5. What mark is placed after the second statement?
6. What mark is placed after the third statement?

Every sentence should begin with a **capital letter.**
A **period** should be placed after every complete statement.

Example: The wind blows the leaves.

EXERCISE

1. Write a statement telling where the sun rises. _____

_____

_____

2. Write a statement telling where the sun sets. _____

_____

_____

3. Write a statement telling in what direction the sun appears to move. _____

_____

_____

4. Write a statement telling one thing that the sun gives us. _____

_____

_____

5. Write a statement telling another thing that the sun gives us. _____

_____

_____

_____

Lesson 3
ORAL COMPOSITION: "THE WIND AND THE SUN"

THE WIND AND THE SUN

The North Wind and the Sun had a dispute as to which of the two was the stronger. While they were talking, a traveller came in sight, and they agreed that the one should be called stronger who first made the traveller take off his cloak.

The North Wind first tried his power, and blew with all his might; but the keener his blasts, the more closely the traveller wrapped his cloak around himself. At last, giving up all hope of victory, he called upon the Sun to make a trial of his strength.

Then the Sun shone out with all his warmth. As soon as the traveller felt the intense heat of the Sun, he loosened his cloak, and soon flung it aside, hastening for protection to the nearest shade.

EXERCISE

Without looking back at the book, tell in your own words the story of "The Wind and the Sun."

Lesson 4
QUESTIONS

The horses ran away.
What made the horses run?
Did they run far?
Was anyone hurt?

1. What is the first sentence about? What is said about the horses?
2. What is the second sentence about?
3. Does the second sentence tell anything about the horses? What does it do?
4. What does the third sentence do?
5. What does the fourth sentence do?
6. Ask something about a watch, about a kite, and about a butterfly.
7. What is a sentence that asks something called?
8. With what kind of letter does the first question begin? What about second question? What about the third question?
9. With what kind of letter should every sentence begin?
10. What mark is placed after the first question? What about second question? What about the third question?

The mark at the end of the above sentences is called a **question mark**.

A question mark (?) should be placed at the end of a question.

Example: Do you like to ride?

EXERCISE 1

Write answers to the following questions. Make each answer a complete statement.

1. Where do we see the moon? _____

_____

2. How often do we have a new moon? _____

_____

3. Where have you seen the new moon at sunset? _____

_____

4. What is the shape of the new moon? _____

_____

5. Where have you seen the full moon at sunset? _____

_____

6. Where do you see the full moon later in the evening? _____

_____

7. In what direction does the moon appear to move? _____

_____

EXERCISE 2

On a separate piece of paper, draw a picture of the new moon.

Lesson 5
MEMORIZATION: "THE MOON"

Read the following poem and commit it to memory.

THE MOON
The moon has a face like the clock in the hall:
She shines on thieves on the garden wall,
On streets and fields and harbor quays,
And birdies asleep in the forks of the trees.

The squalling cat and the squeaking mouse,
The howling dog and the door of the house,
The bat that lies in the bed at noon,
All love to be out by the light of the moon.

But all of the things that belong to the day
Cuddle to sleep to be out of her way;
And flowers and children close their eyes
Till up in the morning the sun shall rise.

Robert Louis Stevenson

The parts into which a poem is divided are called **stanzas**.
Into how many stanzas is this poem divided?

Lesson 6
PICTURE LESSON: "SOAP BUBBLES"

1. How many children do you see in this picture?
2. What is each one doing?
3. Where are the children?
4. What do you see around them?
5. What do you like best about this picture?

EXERCISE

On a separate sheet of paper, write answers to the above questions. Tell about what you see in the picture.

Lesson 7
COMMANDS

1. Give a command that you might use in speaking to a dog.

   Example: **Lie down.**

2. Give a command that you might use in speaking to a person.

   Example: **Close the door.**

3. Give a request that you might make of one of your playmates.

   Example: **Please hold my book.**

4. What request might you make of your teacher or your parents?

EXERCISE 1

On a separate piece of paper, copy the three example commands and requests given above. What mark is placed after each?

A period (.) should be placed after a command or request.

Example: Bring me the notebook.

EXERCISE 2

Tell which of the following sentences state something, which ask something, and which command or request that something be done.

1. Look at the beautiful leaves!
2. Of what colors are the leaves?
3. Name a tree that has red leaves in autumn.
4. Name a tree that has yellow leaves in autumn.
5. Notice how rapidly the leaves fall.
6. What makes the leaves fall from the trees?
7. A few trees hold fast their leaves all winter.

8. What are such trees called?

9. Name two trees that are green throughout the year.

10. What are the leaves of the pine tree often called?

11. Draw a picture of a leaf.

EXERCISE 3

Give a command or request that might be addressed to:

a soldier	a newsboy	a gardener
a sailor	a reader	a fisherman
a carpenter	a singer	a baby

EXERCISE 4

Write a statement telling what your favorite tree is. Tell why you like that tree best.

EXERCISE 5

Draw a picture of a leaf in the space below.

Lesson 8
ORAL COMPOSITION: "THE DOG AND HIS SHADOW"

THE DOG AND HIS SHADOW

A dog, with a piece of meat in his mouth, was crossing a narrow bridge over a stream. Happening to look down into the water, he saw his own shadow, and thought it was another dog with a piece of meat much larger than his own.

He opened his mouth to attack the dog in the water, and so dropped what he had. He thus lost his own piece of meat, which dropped into the water, and the one he wanted, which was only a shadow.

EXERCISE

Tell in your own words the story of "The Dog and His Shadow."

Lesson 9
EXCLAMATIONS

Hark! What bird is that?
Hush! He will hear us.
How sweetly he sings!
What brilliant plumage he has!

1. What does the word *hark* express in the first sentence above?
2. What does the word *hush* express?
3. What word do you sometimes use to express the feeling of pain when something hurts you?
4. What does the third sentence do?
5. How is the fourth sentence used?

A word or sentence that expresses sudden or strong feelings is called an exclamation.

Exclamatory sentences often begin with the words *how* or *what*. For example:

How beautiful the moonlight is!
What a cold winter we have had!

What mark is placed after each exclamation above?

An exclamation should be followed by an exclamation point (!).

Example: Ouch! You stepped on my big toe!

EXERCISE 1

Copy these sentences, then draw a line under each exclamation.

1. Alas! What have I done? ————————————————————

————————————————————————————————

2. Hurrah! Our side has won! ————————————————————

————————————————————————————————

3. There! I have spilled my ink. ————————————————————

————————————————————————————————

4. Hello! Where are you going? ————————————————————

————————————————————————————————

5. Halt! Who goes there? ————————————————————

————————————————————————————————

6. Ah! There he goes! ————————————————————

————————————————————————————————

EXERCISE 2

Change the these sentences from statements to exclamations. Place the right mark after each.

1. The children are happy. ————————————————————

————————————————————————————————

2. The stars are bright. ———————————————————

———————————————————————————————

3. I should like to go. ———————————————————

———————————————————————————————

4. This knife is dull. ———————————————————

———————————————————————————————

5. The boy rides well. ———————————————————

———————————————————————————————

6. We had a hard frost. ———————————————————

———————————————————————————————

7. This room is cold. ———————————————————

———————————————————————————————

8. He must be a wonderful man. ———————————————

———————————————————————————————

9. The sun is warm. ———————————————————

———————————————————————————————

10. This is a beautiful world. ———————————————

———————————————————————————————

EXERCISE 3

Using some of your spelling words for the week, compose two statements, two questions, two exclamations, and two commands. Be careful to punctuate them correctly.

Statement 1 _____

_____

Statement 2 _____

_____

Question 1 _____

_____

Question 2 _____

_____

Exclamation 1 _____

_____

Exclamation 2 _____

_____

Command 1 _____

_____

Command 2 _____

_____

Lesson 10
THE PARAGRAPH

Notice how the sentences are arranged in "The Dog and His Shadow" on page 12.

> **A series of sentences relating to a particular point or the same subject is called a paragraph.**

Tell how many paragraphs are in "The Wind and the Sun" on page 5, and what each paragraph is about.

Notice the small blank space that is left at the beginning of the first line of a paragraph. When a line is begun in this manner, it is said to be **indented**. When you are writing a story or a letter, the first line of each paragraph should be indented.

EXERCISE

On a separate sheet of paper, copy the story "The Dog and His Shadow" from page 12. Do not forget to indent the first line of each paragraph. Use your best handwriting.

Lesson 11
NOUNS

1. What is your name?
2. What is your father's name?
3. Tell the name of some great person of whom you have heard.
4. What is the name of the place in which you live?
5. Tell the name of some place that you have visited.
6. Name five things that you see in your schoolroom.
7. Give the names of two kinds of flowers, two kinds of trees, two animals, two parts of a house, and two pieces of furniture.

EXERCISE 1

1. Write the names of five things that you eat. _____

_____

2. Write the names of five things that you wear. _____

_____

3. Write the names of five things that you play with. _____

_____

4. Write the names of five things that you saw before school this morning. _____

_____

EXERCISE 2

1. Write the names of two trees used for shade. _____

_____

2. Write the names of two animals whose flesh is used for food. _____

_____

3. Write the names of two things made of iron. _____

_____

4. Write the names of two things that grow in the fields. _____

_____

EXERCISE 3

Write statements telling what the animals named below are covered with.

1. horses _____

2. birds _____

3. porcupines _____

4. sheep _____

5. beavers _____

6. fish _____

7. alligators _____

> **Words that tell the names of people, places or things are called nouns.**

EXERCISE 4

Write answers to the following questions. Write your answers as one paragraph.

What kind of food do cats get for themselves? Why do cats need sharp claws? Of what use is the sheath which covers each claw? How is a cat able to walk without noise? Of what use are a cat's whiskers?

_____

_____

_____

_____

_____

_____

_____

_____

_____

Lesson 12
WRITING THE NAMES OF PEOPLE

Charles Adams is reading.
George Moore is making a kite.
Mary Alice is looking at pictures.

1. Which words in these sentences are names?
2. What boy's name do you find in the first sentence? With what kind of letter does his first name begin? What about his last name?
3. What girl's name do you see in the sentences? With what kind of letter does her name begin?

Nouns that tell the name of a specific person, place or thing are called **proper nouns**.

Proper nouns should begin with a **capital letter**.

EXERCISE 1
Copy the following names of American poets.

1. Henry Wadsworth Longfellow _____

2. John Greenleaf Whittier _____

3. James Russell Lowell _____

4. Oliver Wendell Holmes _____

5. William Cullen Bryant _____

EXERCISE 2
Copy the following names, capitalizing them correctly.

1. abraham lincoln _____

2. socrates _____

3. john bunyun _____

4. william shakespeare _____

Nouns that *do not* tell the name of specific people, places or things are called **common nouns**.

Common nouns should begin with a **lowercase** letter.

EXERCISE 3
Circle the common nouns in the list below (some of these nouns are not correctly capitalized).

dog	mr. brown	matthew
turtle	washington	city

EXERCISE 4
Write a proper noun for each of the common nouns you circled in Exercise 3.
For example, for the common noun horse *you might write* Black Beauty.

_____

_____

_____

Lesson 13
PICTURE LESSON: "WHO'LL BUY A RABBIT?"

1. What are these children looking at?
2. Where are the rabbits?
3. Who carries the basket and why has she come here?
4. Where do you think this little girl got her rabbits, and why does she wish to sell them?
5. How many children are looking at the rabbits?
6. Where do you think they live? What are their names?

EXERCISE

On a separate sheet of paper, write a story about this picture. Tell who the little girl with the basket is, and why she went out to sell rabbits. Tell where she went to sell her rabbits, and what success she had.

Lesson 14
GIVEN NAMES AND SURNAMES

That boy is Charles Taylor.

His brother's name is Henry Arthur Taylor.

He has a sister named Edith Taylor.

John Henry Taylor is their father.

1. What is the name of the boy in the first statement?
2. Whose name is given in the second statement?
3. What girl is mentioned in the third statement?
4. Who is spoken of in the last statement?
5. How is it that all the people mentioned in the sentences have the same last name?

The name that belongs to all the members of the same family is called the family name, last name, or surname.

The part of a name given to a child by his parents is called the given name, first name, or Christian name. The given name is sometimes made up of two words.

EXERCISE

Write answers to the following questions. Make each answer a complete statement.

1. What is you father's surname? _____

_____

2. What was your mother's surname before she married? _____

_____

3. What are the surnames of five families that live near you? ———————————

———————————————————————————————————————

———————————————————————————————————————

4. What is your father's given name? —————————————————————

———————————————————————————————————————

5. What is your mother's given name? ————————————————————

———————————————————————————————————————

6. What is your full name? ———————————————————————————

———————————————————————————————————————

Lesson 15
INITIALS

My father's name is James Richard Wilson.
He writes his name as *James R. Wilson.*
My uncle's name is Charles Henry Ford.
He writes his name as *C. H. Ford.*

1. What does the first sentence tell?
2. What does the second sentence tell?
3. What does *R* stand for? What kind of letter is it? What mark is placed after the letter?
4. Whose name is given in the third sentence? Read the name.
5. What does the fourth sentence tell? What does *C* stand for? What mark is placed after the letter *C*? What does *H* stand for? What mark is placed after the letter *H*?

The first letter of a word is called its **initial** letter.

What is the initial letter of the name *Richard*? What about the name *Charles*? What about the name *Henry*?

When, instead of a word in a name, you write the initial of that word, use a **capital** letter.

Place a **period** (.) after each initial.

EXERCISE 1

Copy these names, and in place of the italicized words write the initials of those words.
For example:

      Edith *Hart* Carter   *should be copied as*   **Edith H. Carter**

1. *Mary* Elizabeth Watkins _____

2. Alice *Carr* Watkins ———————————————————

3. Frank *Richard* King ———————————————————

4. Charles *Frank* Sherwood ———————————————————

5. *Arnold Brooks* Sanford ———————————————————

EXERCISE 2

Write the full names of five people you know.

1. ———————————————————

2. ———————————————————

3. ———————————————————

4. ———————————————————

5. ———————————————————

Write each of those names as the owner writes it.

1. ———————————————————

2. ———————————————————

3. ———————————————————

4. ———————————————————

5. ———————————————————

Lesson 16
MEMORIZATION: "PIRATE STORY"

Read the following lines and commit them to memory.

PIRATE STORY

Three of us afloat in the meadow by the swing,
Three of us abroad in the basket on the lea,
Winds are in the air, they are blowing in the spring,
And waves are on the meadow like the waves there are at sea.

Where shall we adventure today that we're afloat,
Wary of the weather and steering by a star?
Shall it be Africa, a-steering of the boat,
To Providence, or Babylon, or off to Malabar?

Hi! but here's a squadron a-rowing on the sea—
Cattle on the meadow a-charging with a roar!
Quick, and we'll escape them, they're as mad as they can be,
The wicket is the harbor and the garden is the shore.

Robert Louis Stevenson

Lesson 17
THE WORD *I*

My name is Frank Gray.
I live in the city.
Edwin and I are playmates.
Edwin is larger than I am.

1. What name do you see in the first sentence?
2. With what kind of letter does the word *Frank* begin?
3. What is the first letter of Frank's last name? What kind of letter is that?
4. When you speak of yourself, what word do you use instead of your own name?
5. What word is used instead of Frank's name in the second sentence? What about the third sentence? What about the fourth?
6. With what kind of letter is *I* written in those sentences?

The word *I* should be written with a capital letter.

EXERCISE

Copy the following sentences.

1. My name is Laura Bell _____

_____

2. I am eight years old. _____

3. I live in the country. _____

4. Mrs. Cary is my teacher. _____

_____

Lesson 18
SENTENCE COMPOSITION

Write the answers to the following questions. Make each answer a complete statement.

1. What is your name? _____

_____

2. How old are you? _____

_____

3. Where do you live? _____

_____

4. What is the name of one or both of your parents? _____

_____

5. Who is your teacher? _____

_____

Lesson 19
NAMES OF CITIES AND STREETS

Harry Graham lives in Boston.
He lives on Beacon Street.
My cousin lives in New York City.

1. What does the first statement tell?
2. What is the name of the city in which Harry lives?
3. With what kind of letter does the word *Boston* begin? Copy the word *Boston*.
4. What does the second statement tell?
5. With what kind of letter does the word *Beacon* begin?
6. With what kind of letter does the word *street* begin? Copy the name of the street on which Harry lives.
7. What city is mentioned in the third statement?
8. How many words are there in the name of that city? With what kind of letter does each word in the name begin? Write *New York City*.

_____

_____

_____

EXERCISE 1
Copy the following names of cities and streets.

Washington _____   Philadelphia _____

Elm Street _____   San Francisco _____

Fifth Avenue _____   Chicago _____

State Street _____   Broadway _____

31

EXERCISE 2

1. Write the name of the city or town in which you live. _____

2. Write the names of two of the leading business streets in your town or city. _____

_____

_____

3. Write the names of three residential streets in your city or town. _____

_____

_____

4. Write the name of the largest city you have visited. _____

Lesson 20
WRITTEN COMPOSITION: CITIES AND CAPITALS

Write answers to the following questions. Make each answer a complete statement.

1. What is the capital of the United States? _____

_____

2. What is the capital of the state in which you live? _____

_____

3. What is the largest city in your state? _____

_____

4. What is the largest city in the United States? _____

_____

5. What is the largest city in the world? _____

_____

Lesson 21
WRITTEN COMPOSITION: "THE LION AND THE MOUSE"

THE LION AND THE MOUSE

One day, as the lion lay sleeping, a mouse ran across his nose and woke him up. The lion laid his paw on the mouse, and was about to crush him, but the mouse begged so hard for his life that the lion let him go.

Not long after, the lion was caught in a net laid by some hunters. He roared and struggled, but his struggles only fastened him more firmly in the net. Just then, up came the little mouse. He went to work gnawing the ropes, and in a short time set the lion free.

1. What took place once when the lion was sleeping?
2. What did the lion do when he saw the mouse?
3. Why did he let the mouse go?
4. What happened to the lion afterward?
5. How did the mouse repay the kindness of the lion?

EXERCISE

On a separate sheet of paper, write the story of "The Lion and the Mouse." First write the subject of the story, then write the story in your own words.

Lesson 22
NAMES OF DAYS

Sunday	**Tuesday**	**Thursday**	**Saturday**
Monday	**Wednesday**	**Friday**	

1. How many days are there in a week?
2. Name the days of the week.
3. With what kind of letter does the name of each day begin?

The names of the days of the week begin with capital letters.

EXERCISE 1

Copy the names of the days of the week.

1. _____   5. _____

2. _____   6. _____

3. _____   7. _____

4. _____

EXERCISE 2

On a separate sheet of paper, write the days of the week in order, from memory.

EXERCISE 3

Write seven statements, in each telling one thing you did on a specific day last week.
For example, "Last Sunday I went to church," or "I lost my knife on Monday."

1. _____

_____

2. _____

_____

3. _____

_____

4. _____

_____

5. _____

_____

6. _____

_____

7. _____

_____

_____

Lesson 23
PICTURE LESSON: "THE FLOOD"

1. What do you see in this picture?
2. Where are they?
3. How did the dog's house come to be floating in the water?
4. What is the mother dog doing?
5. How many puppies are there and what are they doing?

EXERCISE

Write a story about this dog and her puppies.

Lesson 24
NAMES OF MONTHS

January	July
February	August
March	September
April	October
May	November
June	December

Mention in order the names of the months. With what kind of letter does the name of each month begin?

The names of the months should begin with capital letters.

EXERCISE 1
Copy the names of the months.

_____   _____

_____   _____

_____   _____

_____   _____

_____   _____

_____   _____

EXERCISE 2

Copy the following lines, and commit them to memory.

Thirty days hath September,
April, June, and November;
All the rest have thirty-one,
Save February, which alone
Hath twenty-eight; and one day more
We add to it one year in four.

Lesson 25
ABBREVIATIONS OF NAMES OF MONTHS

The names of the months are sometimes shortened, or **abbreviated**, as follows:

January	Jan.
February	Feb.
March	Mar.
April	Apr.
May	May
June	Jun.
July	Jul.
August	Aug.
September	Sept.
October	Oct.
November	Nov.
December	Dec.

The shortened form of a word is called an **abbreviation**.
What mark is placed after each of the foregoing abbreviations?

A period (.) should be placed after an abbreviation.

The abbreviations above are chiefly used in writing dates. The word *May* is never abbreviated, and *March*, *April*, *June*, and *July* are usually written in full.

EXERCISE
On a separate sheet of paper, write from memory the names of the months in order. Opposite each month, write its abbreviation. In those cases where the full form of the month is preferred, write the full form of the word.

Lesson 26
MEMORIZATION: "THE MONTHS"

On a separate sheet of paper, copy this poem and commit it to memory.

THE MONTHS
January brings the snow,
Makes our feet and fingers glow.

February brings the rain,
Thaws the frozen lake again.

March brings breezes loud and shrill,
Stirs the dancing daffodil.

April brings the primrose sweet,
Scatters daisies at our feet.

May brings flocks of pretty lambs,
Skipping by their fleecy dams.

June brings tulips, lilies, roses
Fills the children's hands with posies.

Hot July brings cooling showers,
Apricots and gillyflowers.

August brings the sheaves of corn,
Then the harvest home is borne.

Warm September brings the fruit,
Sportsmen then begin to shoot.

Fresh October brings the pheasant,
Then to gather nuts is pleasant.

Dull November brings the blast,
Then the leaves are whirling fast.

Chill December brings the sleet,
Blazing fire and Christmas treat.

Sara Coleridge

Lesson 27
DICTATION EXERCISE: MONTHS

On a separate sheet of paper, copy these lines as your teacher reads them aloud.

1. January is the first month in the year.
2. February is the shortest month in the year.
3. March brings cold winds.
4. April showers bring May flowers.
5. June is the month of roses.
6. September is the harvest month.
7. October brings bright red and yellow leaves.
8. Christmas comes in December.

Lesson 28
SEASONS

1. What flowers blossom in the spring?
2. What do you see on fruit trees?
3. What do the birds do in spring?
4. What does the farmer plant?
5. What kind of weather do we have in summer?
6. What insects do you see flying about?
7. What fruits ripen in the summer months?
8. What are the colors of the leaves in the early part of autumn?
9. What becomes of the leaves later?
10. What does the farmer harvest in autumn?
11. What kind of weather do we have in winter? What sometimes covers the ground?
12. Why are little streams said to be asleep in winter?
13. Name some of the winter sports.

The names of the seasons usually begin with lowercase letters.

EXERCISE 1

Write answers to the following questions about spring.

1. What signs of spring have you noticed? _____

_____

_____

2. Which birds came first, and when did they arrive? _____

_____

3. When did you see the first butterfly? _____

4. What are some of the earliest wildflowers? Which blossom first? _____

_____

_____

5. Which trees leaf out first in the spring? _____

_____

_____

EXERCISE 2

Write answers to the following questions about summer.

1. What are some of the common fruits of summer? Which ripen first? _____

_____

_____

2. Which fruits are your favorites? _____

_____

3. What are your favorite flowers that blossom in summer? _____

_____

_____

EXERCISE 3

Write answers to the following questions about autumn.

1. What birds leave your area in autumn? _____

_____

2. What flowers blossom in the autumn months? _____

_____

3. What nuts ripen at this time? _____

_____

4. Which wild animals are common? _____

_____

EXERCISE 4

Write answers to the following questions about winter.

1. What have you noticed about the length of the days in winter? _____

_____

2. What holidays come in the winter months? _____

_____

3. Which season do you like best, and why do you like it best? _____

_____

_____

Lesson 29
ORAL COMPOSITION: "THE ANTS AND THE GRASSHOPPER"

THE ANTS AND THE GRASSHOPPER

In a large field filled with grasshoppers, there lived a family of ants. The ants were busy all day gathering grain for winter's use. When winter arrived, a grasshopper, half-dead with hunger, came and begged the ants for food.

"Why did you not store up food during the summer?" asked the ants.

The grasshopper replied, "I have to spend my time in singing."

The ants then said, "If you were foolish enough to sing all the summer, you must dance hungry to bed in the winter."

EXERCISE

Tell in your own words the story of "The Ants and the Grasshopper."

Lesson 30
MEMORIZATION: "SONG OF THE GRASS BLADES"

SONG OF THE GRASS BLADES
Peeping, peeping, here and there,
In lawns and meadows everywhere,
Coming up to find the spring,
And hear the robin redbreast sing;
Creeping under children's feet,
Glancing at the violets sweet,
Growing into tiny bowers,
For the dainty meadow flowers:
We are small, but think a minute
Of a world with no grass in it!

Author Unknown

1. At what time of year does the grass come up?
2. What is meant by the grass blades "peeping" here and there?
3. Where have you seen the grass blades come up?
4. Do you like to think of a world with no grass in it?

EXERCISE
Copy the "Song of the Grass Blades" on a separate sheet of paper, and commit it to memory.

Lesson 31
PICTURE LESSON: "SHOEING THE HORSE"

EXERCISE 1

Write answers to these questions about the picture.

1. What does this picture represent? _____

_____

2. What is a man who shoes horses called? _____

3. What is the room where he works called? _____

4. How do you like this horse? Why do you think he stands so quietly to be shod?

_____

_____

5. What kind of disposition has he? What makes you think so? _____

_____

_____

6. What other animals do you see in this shop? What else do you see in it? _____

_____

7. What do all these things tell you about the blacksmith? _____

_____

_____

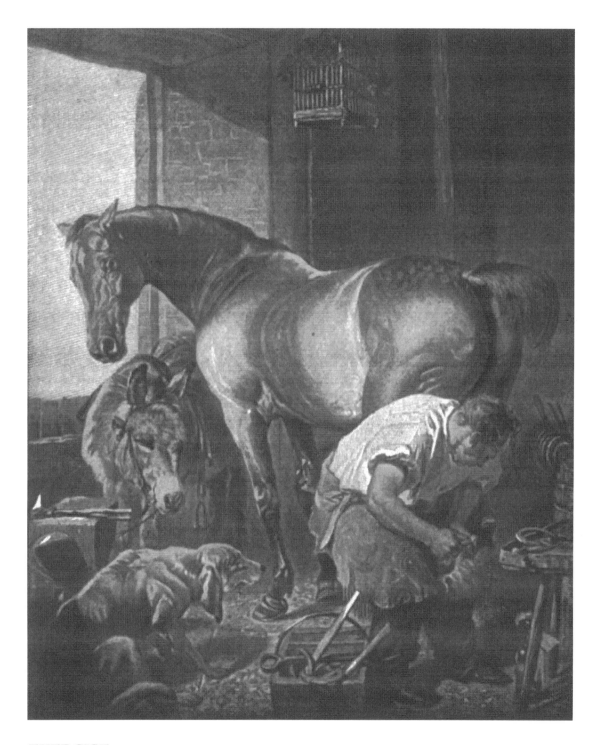

EXERCISE 2

Write a story about this horse. Describe him, and tell his name. Tell who his master is, what kind of home the horse has, and what he does. Tell where he went one day and what happened.

Lesson 32
TITLES

Mr. (Mister)	Mrs. (Mistress)
Master	Miss

Which of the titles above are abbreviated? Which are written in full?

Mr. and *Mrs.* are titles used before names as a mark of respect and courtesy. *Mr.* is used before the name of a man, and *Mrs.* (pronounced *Missis*) before the name of a married woman. These titles are abbreviated forms of *Mister* and *Mistress*, and we almost always write the abbreviated forms.

The title *Master* is used before the name of a boy in very formal situations. The title *Miss* is prefixed to the name of a girl or unmarried woman. If you do not know whether a woman is married or unmarried, you may use the abbreviation *Ms.* (pronounced *Miz*). The titles *Master* and *Miss* are always written in full.

EXERCISE
Copy the following names. Do not forget to place a period after each abbreviation.

1. **Mrs. Elizabeth Barrett Browning** _____

_____

2. **Mr. Charles Dudley Warner** _____

_____

3. **Mr. John Burroughs** _____

4. **Miss Florence Dombey** _____

5. **Master Paul Dombey** _____

Lesson 33
AUNTS AND UNCLES

Aunt Clara brought me a watch.
It was a present from Uncle William.

1. What is told in the first sentence? Who brought the watch?
2. Copy the name *Aunt Clara* below.
3. Read the second sentence. Who sent the watch?
4. Copy the name *Uncle William* below. With what kind of letter does *uncle* begin?
5. Give the name of one of your uncles. When you speak to your uncle, what do you call him? Write that name below.
7. Tell the name of one of your aunts. What do you call her? Write that name below.

_____

_____

_____

_____

> **When you write the word *uncle* or the word *aunt* as part of a name, begin it with a capital letter.**
>
> **Example: My Aunt May fell through the floor today.**

EXERCISE

On a separate sheet of paper, write about a visit to your aunt's home. Begin as follows:

My visit to Aunt _____'s house.

Tell where your aunt lives, when you visited her, and what you did while you were there.

Lesson 34
WRITING DATES

Abraham Lincoln was the sixteenth president of the United States.

He was born February 12, 1809.

He died April 15, 1865.

1. Who was Abraham Lincoln?
2. In what month was he born? On what day of the month? In what year?
3. In what year did he die?
4. How do you know, from the third sentence, on what day of the month he died?
5. How is the day of the month written? How is the year written?
6. What mark separates the figures which tell the day of the month from those which give the year?

In the dates above, *12* and *15* are abbreviations of *twelfth* and *fifteenth*. These dates should not be read as *February twelve* and *April fifteen*, but *February twelfth* and *April fifteenth*.

EXERCISE 1

Read the following dates aloud correctly, and notice how they are written.

October 12, 1492   April 30, 1789

December 21, 1620   June 17, 1800

February 22, 1732   September 12, 1966

April 22, 1732   January 1, 2000

July 4, 1776   December 25, 2004

EXERCISE 2

Copy the following sentences, filling in the blanks where necessary.

1. Columbus discovered America on October 12, 1492. _____

_____

2. The Pilgrims landed at Plymouth on December 21, 1620. _____

_____

_____

3. George Washington was born February 22, 1732. _____

_____

4. I was born _____ _____ , _____ . _____
                MONTH   **DAY**   **YEAR**

_____

5. Today is _____ _____ , _____ . _____
             MONTH   **DAY**   **YEAR**

_____

Lesson 35
WRITING A LETTER

Look carefully at the letter at the bottom of the page, noticing its different parts. First comes the **heading**, which shows where the letter was written and when it was written. Next is the **salutation**, consisting of the opening words. Then follows the **body** of the letter, containing what is said in the letter. Lastly comes the **conclusion**, which is made up of the closing words and **signature** of the writer.

EXERCISE

Copy this letter on a separate sheet of paper. Notice how the different parts are arranged, and place them in the same way.

Albany, New York
October 14, 2004

Dear Eva,
    I have two little kittens. Their names are Buff and Gold.
    Buff follows me wherever I go. When I sit down, she climbs into my lap and purrs softly.
    Gold is afraid to come without an invitation. She rubs against my feet, and looks up into my face longingly. Then I say, "Come, Gold!" and she jumps into my lap, and curls down by Buff.
    Will you not come and see my kittens?

Your Friend,

Emily Hall

Lesson 36
WRITTEN COMPOSITION: A LETTER

Write a letter to one of your playmates. Tell about something that you have at home. Begin and close your letter like the example given on the preceding page. In your letter, use the name of the city or town in which you live, your own name, and the name of one of your friends.

Lesson 37
WRITING ADDRESSES

The address of a person is made up of his name and his place of residence.

When the words *street* or *avenue* occur in addresses, they are usually abbreviated.

Street *is written as* **St.**   **Avenue** *is written as* **Ave.**

1. Read the first address in this lesson. Whose address is it?
2. What word is placed before Walter's name?
3. On what street does Walter live? What is the number of his house?
4. In what city does he live? In what state?
5. Read the second address. What word is placed before Hilary Barton's name?
6. What does the second line of the address tell?
7. What does the third line tell?
8. If you were writing your mother's address on an envelope, what would you place before her name?
9. If you were writing your father's address, what would you place before his name?

EXERCISE I

Draw two rectangles on a sheet of paper, making each rectangle the shape and size of a small envelope. Make each figure about 5 ¹/₂ inches long and 3 ¹/₄ inches wide. Or, lay an envelope on the paper and trace around it.

In those rectangles, copy the two addresses given at the beginning of this lesson. In each, write the first line of the address near the middle of the figure, and be careful to place the other lines just as they are placed in the models given. Use commas and periods as they are used in the addresses given. Mark the place for the postage stamp.

EXERCISE 2

1. Write your own address as it should be written on an envelope. Write your full name, not your nickname.

_____

_____

_____

2. Write the address of your parents or of your guardian.

_____

_____

_____

3. Write the address of one of your playmates.

_____

_____

_____

Lesson 38
WRITTEN COMPOSITION: LETTERS

EXERCISE 1

Write a letter from Julian to Louis.

If tomorrow is a pleasant day, Willis and Julian are going to take their tent and camp out in the maple grove. They would like to have Louis go with them. Willis will carry their dinner in his father's old knapsack. Julian will take along his new book, Hans Brinker, *and he would like Louis to take his bow and arrow with him. On a separate sheet of paper, write the letter for Julian.*

EXERCISE 2

Write a reply from Louis to Julian.

Louis would like nothing better than to camp out with Julian and Willis. He will go, and will take his bow and arrow with him. On a separate sheet of paper, write the letter for Louis.

EXERCISE 3

Write a letter from Ruth to Bertha.

It was so warm today that Ruth went out to look at the pansies in her flower bed. She found the snow all gone, and the pansies in blossom. She sends some pansies to Bertha by way of Frank. On a separate sheet of paper, write the letter for Ruth.

EXERCISE 4

Write a reply from Bertha to Ruth.

Bertha thanks Ruth for the pansies. She thinks they are beautiful, and she has put them into her little Japanese cup. She sends Ruth her latest copy of Highlights. *On a separate sheet of paper, write the letter for Bertha.*

Lesson 39
PICTURE LESSON: "MAKING THE CROSSBOW"

EXERCISE

On a separate piece of paper, write answers to these questions.

1. What do you see in this picture?
2. What is the man doing?
3. Why are the children so interested in his work?
4. What other person do you see in the room?
5. Why does she not watch the making of the cross-bow?
6. What do you think the man will do with the cross-bow when it is finished?

Lesson 40
IS AND *ARE*

> Herbert is in the house.
> Herbert and Alfred are in the house.
> The pencil is dull.
> The pencils are dull.

1. Who is spoken of in the first statement?
2. Who is spoken of in the second statement?
3. Why do we use the word *is* in the first statement and *are* in the second statement?
4. What is the third statement about? How many pencils are spoken of?
5. What is the fourth statement about?
6. Which word is used in stating something about one pencil, *is* or *are*?
7. What word is used instead of *is* when speaking of more than one pencil?

Look again at the sentences given in this lesson, and tell when we use the word *is*. Tell when we use the word *are*.

Use the word *is* when speaking of one person or thing.
Use the word *are* when speaking of more than one person or thing.

EXERCISE

Copy the following sentences, filling in the blanks with is *or* are. *Be careful to use* is *in statements about one, and* are *in statements about more than one.*

1. The bell _____ ringing. _____

2. The sweet apples _____ ripe. _____

3. _____ your brother at home? _____

60

4. ———— your sisters here? ————————————————————

5. The birds ———— singing. ————————————————————

6. The eggs of the phoebe-bird ———— snow-white. ————————————

————————————————————————————————————

7. The asters and the goldenrod ———— in blossom. ————————————

————————————————————————————————————

8. The whale ———— the largest animal in the world. ————————————

————————————————————————————————————

9. The elephant ———— the largest animal that lives upon land. ————————

————————————————————————————————————

————————————————————————————————————

10. The bison or buffalo ———— the largest animal in North America. ————————

————————————————————————————————————

————————————————————————————————————

Lesson 41
DICTATION EXERCISE

On a separate sheet of paper, copy these sentences down as your teacher reads them aloud.

1. What is this little green tip peeping up out of the ground under the snowy covering?
2. It is a young snowdrop plant.
3. Can you tell me why it grows?
4. Where does it find its food?
5. What makes it spread out its leaves and add length to its stalk day by day?

Lesson 42
WRITTEN COMPOSITION: "THE CROW AND THE PITCHER"

THE CROW AND THE PITCHER

A crow, perishing with thirst, saw a pitcher and flew to it, hoping to find water there. He found a little water in the bottom of the pitcher, but it was so low that he could not reach it. He looked around to see what he could do, and spied some pebbles.

He brought these, one by one, and dropped them into the pitcher until the water was brought within his reach.

1. What did the crow see?
2. Why did he fly to it?
3. What was the reason he could not get water there?
4. What did he do?

EXERCISE

On a separate sheet of paper, write in your own words the story of "The Crow and the Pitcher."

Lesson 43
WAS AND *WERE*

Agnes was in the garden.
Agnes and Alice were in the garden.
The bird was shy.
The birds were shy.

1. Who is spoken of in the first sentence?
2. Who is spoken of in the second sentence?
3, In which sentence is the word *was* used?
4. What word is used instead of *was* in the second sentence?
5. Why is the word *was* used in the first sentence and *were* in the second sentence?
6. What is the third sentence about? How many birds are spoken of?
7. Tell whether we use the word *was* or *were* to state something about one bird.
8. What is the fourth sentence about? What word is used instead of *was* in stating something about the birds?
9. In which of the sentences above is the word *was* used? How many things are spoken of in each of those sentences?
10. What word do we use instead of *was* when we speak of more than one?

Use *was* when speaking of one.
Use *were* when speaking of more than one.

EXERCISE
Copy the following sentences, filling in the blanks with is, are, was, *or* were.

1. Carlo _____ lonesome. _____

2. Fred and Harry _____ away. _____

3. _____ those marbles yours? _____

64

4. The ground _____ covered with snow. _____

_____

5. Horses _____ first brought to America by Spanish explorers. _____

_____

_____

6. The llama lives on the Andes. It _____ much larger than a sheep, and it _____ covered with long, soft brown or gray hair.

_____

_____

_____

Lesson 44
REVIEW

EXERCISE 1

Complete these oral compositions verbally.

1. Use the word *is* in asking a question about an animal, then a question about a flower.
2. Use the word *are* in making a statement about yourself and a playmate. Mention yourself last.
3. Use the word *was* in asking a question about a river, then a question about the wind.
4. Use the word *were* in asking a question about the stars.
5. Use the word *were* in making a statement about two boys.

EXERCISE 2

Answer these questions verbally.

1. When should you use the word *was*?
2. When should you use the word *were*?
3. What is a sentence that states something called?
4. What is a sentence that asks something called?
5. What mark should be placed after a statement?
6. What mark should be placed after a question?
7. What mark should be placed after a command?
8. What mark should be placed after an exclamation?
9. With what kind of a letter should you begin each word in your name?
10. How should you write the word *I*?

EXERCISE 3

Fill the blanks with is, are, was, *or* were.

1. The boy _____ waiting for the basket.

2. The leaves _____ falling.

3. A pigeon _____ walking on the roof.

66

4. Two pigeons ———— walking on the roof.

5. The larks ———— ground birds when they perch, and ———— sky birds when they sing.

6. Have you ever lifted a stone that had ants under it and seen the ants hurry away, carrying little, roundish white things to some safe place? People will tell you that

these little white things ———— ants' eggs, but they ———— not.

7. They ———— little white silk cocoons, and the baby ants ———— inside them.

Lesson 45
ORAL COMPOSITION: "THE BATTLE OF THE FROGS AND MICE"

THE BATTLE OF THE FROGS AND MICE

A mouse had been chased by a weasel and had just escaped, very tired and thirsty. He was drinking from the edge of a pond when Puffcheek, the king of the frogs, asked the stranger his name and the name of his father. The mouse said that his name was Crumbstealer, and that he was the son of Breadgnawer.

Then Puffcheek, the king of the frogs, invited the mouse, Crumbstealer, to his house, and offered to carry him there on his back. So Crumbstealer jumped on to Puffcheek's back, and they started merrily off across the water.

When they had gotten out to where the water was deep, what should they see but a great green snake. It lifted up its head just in front of Puffcheek, and Puffcheek dived to the bottom, without stopping to think of Crumbstealer on his back. And so poor Crumbstealer, who could not swim, was left to drown.

Now another mouse, Lickplatter, was sitting on the bank of the pond, and saw all that happened. So he told the other mice, and they were all very angry. They said that Puffcheek had taken Crumbstealer out into the middle of the pond and drowned him, and they declared war on the frogs. They made breastplate out of the skin of a weasel, carried skewers for spears, and wore nutshells for helmets.

Then the frogs met together in council. Puffcheek told the other frogs that he had had nothing to do with the death of Crumbstealer, but that Crumbstealer had drowned himself while trying to swim like a frog.

So the frogs went out to meet the mice in battle. They carried radish leaves for shields, and rushes for spears, and wore snail shells for helmets. Then there was terrible fighting, and many mighty deeds were done on both sides.

All the frogs would have been slain, if Jupiter had not interfered by sending an army of fearful monsters to their aid. These creatures had eight feet and two heads; their mouths were like shears and their eyes were set in their breasts. Men called them crabs.

When these frightful creatures came against the mice, pinching their tails and breaking their spears, the mice turned and fled in terror. And so the great battle ended, and the sun went down.

EXERCISE

Tell about "The Battle of the Frogs and Mice" in your own words.

Lesson 46
HAS AND HAVE

A squirrel has sharp teeth.
Squirrels have sharp teeth.
The boy has gone home.
The boys have gone home.

1. What is the first statement about? What is said about the squirrel?
2. What is the second statement about?
3. Which of these sentences states something about one thing?
4. Which of them states something about more than one thing?
5. Why is the word *has* used in the first statement and *have* in the second?
6. Read the third and fourth sentences. In which of these sentences is *has* used? Why?
7. In which is the word *have* used? Why?

Use *has* in speaking of one.
Use *have* in speaking of more than one.

EXERCISE 1

Fill the blanks with has, have, is, *or* are.

1. A true insect _____ a body divided into three parts.

2. All insects _____ six legs. Most insects _____ four wings.

3. Spiders _____ eight legs, and no wings.

4. The body of a spider _____ divided into two parts.

5. The spider _____ not a true insect.

EXERCISE 2

Write the answers to the following questions. Make each answer a complete statement.

1. Into how many parts is the body of a fly divided? _____

_____

2. How many legs has a fly? _____

_____

3. How many wings has a fly? _____

_____

4. Is the fly a true insect? _____

_____

5. Into how many parts is the body of a bee divided? _____

_____

6. How many legs has a bee? _____

_____

7. How many wings has a bee? _____

_____

8. Is the bee a true insect? _____

_____

Lesson 47
WRITTEN COMPOSITION: PETS

Write something about your pet(s). If you have pigeons or a canary, a dog, a cat, or rabbits, write answers to one of the sets of questions below. If you have none of the pets named in this lesson, write about the one(s) you do have. Write carefully, and be sure to begin every sentence with a capital letter. Write your essay on a separate sheet of paper.

QUESTIONS ABOUT PIGEONS

1. How many pigeons have you?
2. Where do they stay?
3. What kind of house do they live in? Where is it?
4. What do they eat?
5. Are they tame?
6. Will they eat out of your hands, and light on your shoulders?
7. How do the old pigeons teach the young ones to fly?
8. What do pigeons do when they are happy?
9. Tell a little story about your pigeons.

QUESTIONS ABOUT CANARIES

1. How old is your canary?
2. Of what color is it?
3. What is its name?
4. Who takes care of it?
5. What do you do for it?
6. What does it eat?
7. How often does it take a bath?
8. How does the bird answer when you talk to it?
9. Where do you keep its cage?
10. During what part of the day does it sing the most?
11. How does it sit when it sleeps?
12. Tell a little story about your canary.

QUESTIONS ABOUT DOGS

1. What kind of dog have you?
2. What is its name?
3. Where does it sleep at night?
4. How does it welcome you when you come home?
5. How does it act when strangers come to the house?
6. Has it any interesting tricks or habits? What are they?
7. Tell a little story about your dog.

QUESTIONS ABOUT CATS

1. What is your cat's name?
2. What color is the cat?
3. What do you feed it?
4. What food does it get for itself?
5. How does it catch a mouse?
6. What does it do with the mouse before it kills it?
7. Where does your cat like to lie best?
8. What does it do when it is happy?
9. Tell a little story about your cat.

QUESTIONS ABOUT RABBITS

1. How many rabbits have you?
2. Where did you get them?
3. How old are they?
4. What do you call them?
5. Where do you keep them?
6. What do they like to eat?
7. How did you tame them?
8. Tell some interesting thing that they do.
9. Tell a little story about your rabbits.

Lesson 48
WORDS TO USE WITH *YOU*

Has John a pencil?
Have the boys pencils?

1. About whom is the first question asked?
2. If you spoke to John and asked him the first question, what would you say?
3. Read the second question. What would you say if you were asking the boys that question?
4. Did you use *has* or *have* with the word *you* when it meant one person?
5. Did you use *has* or *have* with the word *you* when it meant more than one?

EXERCISE 1

Change these questions. Do not speak about the boys, but speak to them. Write the question that you would ask.

1. **Where is John going?** _____

_____

2. **Where are the boys going?** _____

_____

Did you use *is* or *are* in your first question?
Which of those words did you use in your second question?

EXERCISE 2

Change these questions. Do not speak about the boys, but speak to them. Write the question that you would ask.

1. **Where was John last night?** _____

74

2. **Where were the boys last night?** _____

_____

What did you say in asking John the first question? What did you say in asking the boys the second question? Did you use *was* or *were* with the word *you* in your first question? Did you use *was* or *were* with the word *you* in your second question?

With the word *you*, should we use *has* or *have*? *is* or *are*? *was* or *were*?

Use the words *have*, *are*, and *were* with the word *you*, whether it refers one or more than one.

EXERCISE 3

1. Write a statement using the word *you* with the word *have*. _____

_____

_____

2. Write a statement using the word *you* with the word *are*. _____

_____

_____

3. Write a statement using the word *you* with the word *were*. _____

_____

_____

4. Write a question using the word *you* with the word *have.* _____

_____

_____

5. Write a question using the word *you* with the word *are.* _____

_____

_____

6. Write a question using the word *you* with the word *were.* _____

_____

_____

Lesson 49
PICTURE LESSON: "THE BABY SITTER"

Write a story suggested by this picture. Tell who this little girl is, where she is, and what she is doing. Tell whose baby this is, and what the little girl does to make her happy.

Lesson 50
QUOTATION MARKS

"Come and see the morning glories," said Henry.
"Do they blossom every morning?" asked Ida.
"Yes," answered Henry.
"Let's count the blossoms," said Ida.

1. Whose words are repeated in the first sentence?
2. Read the part of the first sentence that tells what Henry said.
3. What question did Ida ask? Read her exact words.

When the exact words of a person are repeated by another person, they are said to be **quoted**. The words repeated are called **direct quotations**.

4. What words are quoted in the second sentence?
5. Notice the little marks that are placed before and after Ida's words.
   How are they made?

The little marks (" ") that enclose the exact words used by another person are called **quotation marks**.

Every **direct quotation** should be enclosed by **quotation marks**.

---

6. Read the third sentence. Why is the word *yes* enclosed by quotation marks?
7. Whose words are repeated in the fourth sentence?
8. Read Ida's words. What are the marks called that enclose her words?

EXERCISE 1

Copy the four sentences at the beginning of this lesson.

1. _____

_____

2. _____

_____

3. _____

4. _____

_____

EXERCISE 2

Copy the following sentences on a separate sheet of paper, placing quotation marks wherever they are needed.

> The red rose says, Be sweet,
> And the lily bids, Be pure;
> The hardy, brave chrysanthemum,
> Be patient and endure;
> The violet whispers, Give,
> Nor grudge nor count the cost:
> The woodbine, Keep on blossoming
> In spite of chill and frost.
>
> *Susan Coolidge.*

Lesson 51
THE COMMA WITH QUOTATIONS

George said to Robert, "Where is Bruno?"
Robert replied, "He is in the barn."

1. To whom did George speak?
2. What did he say?
3. Read the second sentence. Whose words are repeated in this sentence?
4. What shows that the words are quoted?
5. What mark is placed before the quotation in each sentence?
6. With what kind of letter does the first word of each quoted sentence begin?

A **short direct quotation** should be separated from the remainder of the sentence by a **comma (,)**.

The first word of a **quotation** should begin with a **capital** letter.

EXERCISE 1
Underline the quotations in the following story.

THE FARMER AND THE STORK
A farmer set a net in his field, to catch the cranes which came to feed on his corn. He caught several cranes, and with them a stork.

The stork begged the farmer to let him go. He said, "I am not a wicked crane, but a poor, harmless stork."

The farmer replied, "That may be true, but I have caught you with the cranes, and you must die with them."

EXERCISE 2
Tell the story of "The Farmer and the Stork" in your own words.

Lesson 52
DICTATION EXERCISE: "THE FOX AND THE GRAPES"

On a separate sheet of paper, copy this story down as your teacher reads it aloud. Your teacher will read it to you all the way through once, then one phrase at a time.

THE FOX AND THE GRAPES

A hungry Fox saw some bunches of ripe grapes hanging from a vine, high up from the ground. He tried different ways to get them, but wearied himself in vain, for he could not reach them. At last he turned away, muttering, "The grapes are sour, and not as ripe as I thought."

Lesson 53
WRITTEN COMPOSITION: "THE FOX AND THE CROW"

THE FOX AND THE CROW

A crow stole a piece of cheese and flew with it to a tall tree. A fox, seeing the crow and wishing to get the cheese for himself, tried to obtain it through flattery.

"What a beautiful bird you are! What glossy feathers you have!" he exclaimed. "If your voice were only equal to your beauty, you would surely be called the Queen of Birds!"

The crow, highly pleased, opened her mouth to caw, and down dropped the cheese. The fox quickly picked it up and ran off.

EXERCISE 1
Tell the story in your own words.

EXERCISE 2
In you own words, write the story of "The Fox and the Crow." Be careful to use quotation marks if you give the exact words of the fox and the crow. Write your story on a separate sheet of paper.

Lesson 54
THE COMMA IN DIRECT ADDRESS

Horace, look at the falling leaves!
Come, Horace, let us gather the leaves.

1. Who is spoken to in the first sentence?
2. What mark separates the word *Horace* from the rest of the sentence?
3. Where is the name of the person addressed placed in the second sentence?
4. How many commas are used to separate it from the rest of the sentence?

When you speak to a person, you are said to **address** him.

The name of the person addressed should be separated from the rest of the sentence by a **comma** (,) or **commas**.

Examples: "Jane, don't go!" or "Hurry up, Mike, so we can leave."

EXERCISE
Read the following sentences. Insert the omitted commas and quotation marks.

1. Little Red Riding Hood met a wolf, who said to her, Good morning Little Red Riding Hood.

2. Good morning Master Wolf said the little girl.

3. Where are you going? asked the wolf.

4. I am going to my grandmother's, said Little Red Riding Hood.

5. Where does your grandmother live? asked the wolf.

6. On the other side of the wood, said the child.

Lesson 55
DICTATION EXERCISE: "WHERE ARE YOU GOING?"

On a separate sheet of paper, copy these sentences down as your teacher reads them aloud.

1. "Where are you going, my pretty maid?"
2. "I am going a-milking, Sir," she said.
3. "May I go with you, my pretty maid?"
4. "You're kindly welcome, Sir," she said.
5. "What is your father, my pretty maid?"
6. "My father's a farmer, Sir," she said.
7. "What is your fortune, my pretty maid?"
8. "My face is my fortune, Sir," she said.
9. "Then I won't marry you, my pretty maid."
10. "Nobody asked you, Sir," she said.

Lesson 56
ORAL COMPOSITION: "THE TORTOISE AND THE HARE"

THE TORTOISE AND THE HARE

One day a hare made fun of the short legs and slow pace of a tortoise. The tortoise said, "If you will try a race with me, I will beat you." The hare, feeling sure that he could win, consented to try the race. They agreed that the fox should mark out the course and be the judge.

On the day appointed for the race, they started together. The tortoise never stopped for an instant, but went on with a slow, steady pace, straight to the end of the course. The hare, knowing that he could reach the goal with but a few leaps, lay down by the side of the road and fell fast asleep. When the hare awoke, he ran as fast as he could, but soon found that the tortoise had already reached the goal, and was quietly resting.

EXERCISE 2
Tell in your own words the story of "The Tortoise and the Hare."

Lesson 57
CONTRACTIONS

I've torn the book.
Don't be careless.

1. What does the word *I've* mean in the first sentence?
2. Write the words *I have*. Write the word *I've*. What letters are in the words *I have* that are not in the word *I've*?
3. In writing the word *I've*, what do you place where the letters *h* and *a* are left out?

The mark we use to replace omitted letters is called an **apostrophe** (').

4. From what two words is the word *don't* made?
5. Why is the apostrophe used?

Words like *I've* and *don't* are formed from two words, by leaving out one or more letters and replacing them with an apostrophe. These words are called **contractions**.

An apostrophe (') should be used in a contraction wherever one or more letters are left out.

Contractions are often used in casual conversation and writing, but they are seldom used in formal writing.

EXERCISE
Write the contracted words in each sentence in their uncontracted forms.

1. **There's the postman.** _____

2. **Didn't you hear the bell?** _____

3. Don't you like October weather? ——————————

4. Aren't the clouds beautiful? ——————————

5. I can't find the key. ——————————

6. It's on the shelf. ——————————

7. Isn't the room cold? ——————————

8. They're coming to meet us. ——————————

9. Said the cunning Spider to the Fly, ——————————
   "Dear friend, what can I do
    to prove the warm affection
    I've always felt for you."

10. This coat doesn't fit ——————————

Lesson 58
DICTATION EXERCISE

On a separate sheet of paper, copy these sentences down as your teacher reads them aloud.

1. Doesn't the wind blow hard?
2. I'm glad that you're safe at home.
3. Couldn't you row the boat?
4. It's three miles to the river.
5. Here's a young robin.
6. It's the early bird that catches the worm.
7. I've bought a pony. Isn't he a nice one? Wouldn't you like to ride him?
8. Where's the little boy who looks after the sheep?
9. He's under the haystack, fast asleep.

Lesson 59
MEMORIZATION: "THE BROWN THRUSH"

THE BROWN THRUSH

I

There's a merry brown thrush sitting up in the tree;

"He's singing to me! he's singing to me!"

And what does he say, little girl, little boy?

"Oh, the world's running over with joy!

Don't you hear? Don't you see?

Hush! look! in my tree.

I'm as happy as happy can be!"

II

And the brown thrush keeps singing, "A nest do you see,

And five eggs hid by me in the juniper-tree?

Don't meddle! Don't touch! little girl, little boy,

Or the world will lose some of its joy:

Now I'm glad! now I'm free!

And I always shall be,

If you never bring sorrow to me!"

III

So the merry brown thrush sings away in the tree.

To you and to me, to you and to me;

And he sings all the day, little girl, little boy,

"Oh, the world's running over with joy!

But long it won't be,

Don't you know? don't you see?

Unless we are as good as can be."

Lucy Larcom

1. What is sitting in the tree?
2. What is he doing?
3. What does the thrush say in his song?
4. Why was he so happy?
5. Where was the nest of the thrush?
6. How many eggs were in it?
7. What caution is given about the nest?
8. To whom does the thrush sing?
9. What does he say to everybody?
10. Into how many stanzas is this poem divided?
11. With what kind of letter should every line of poetry begin?

EXERCISE 1

Copy "The Brown Thrush" onto a separate sheet of paper and commit it to memory.

EXERCISE 2

Make a list of the contractions in this poem, and opposite each contraction write the words for which it stands.

_____	_____
_____	_____
_____	_____
_____	_____
_____	_____
_____	_____
_____	_____

Lesson 60
PICTURE LESSON: "THE PLAYFUL KITTENS"

1. How many kittens do you see in this picture?
2. What are they doing?
3. Where is the mother cat?

EXERCISE

Write a story about these kittens.

Lesson 61
WRITTEN COMPOSITION: "HOW APOLLO GOT HIS LYRE"

HOW APOLLO GOT HIS LYRE

A child, Mercury, was born in a cave among the mountains. Before he was a day old he climbed out of his crib and ran out into the sunshine.

A pretty spotted tortoise shell lay on the grass near the door of the cave. Mercury, seeing it, brought it inside. Taking hollow reed canes, a piece of leather, and strings, he made a lyre of it. Then he sang and, striking the lyre, made beautiful music all day long.

When it was beginning to grow dark, he stole out of doors again and went to the pastures where Apollo's white cattle were feeding. He chased them back and forth, and drove part of them away off into a cave, and fastened them in. He had chased them in so many directions that their tracks looked as if, instead of going in, they had come out of the cave.

Then he went home, just as the light was coming in the east. He slipped through the keyhole, climbed into his cradle again, and was soon fast asleep with the lyre held fast in his arms.

Now Apollo was Mercury's brother. When he missed his white cows, someone told him that a baby had been seen the night before, driving cattle, and Apollo went straight to the cave where Mercury lay in his cradle.

At first Apollo was angry. But Mercury, sitting in his cradle, his eyes sparkling with fun, played on his lyre and made wonderful music, sweeter than any that had ever been heard before. Apollo was so charmed by the music that he forgave his little brother. Then Mercury told Apollo where his cows were, and gave him the lyre and showed him how to play on it. Apollo, in return, made Mercury his shepherd, and gave him charge of all his flocks and herds so that he might drive them as much as he pleased.

Some days when the wind is blowing, and fleecy white clouds are flying before it over the sky, you may look up and see Mercury driving Apollo's white cattle.

EXERCISE

On a separate sheet of paper, write in your own words "How Apollo Got His Lyre."

Lesson 62
REVIEW

EXERCISE 1
Write statements telling interesting facts about the following things.

1. cork _____

_____

2. pearls _____

_____

3. coal _____

_____

4. bananas _____

_____

5. sponges _____

_____

6. cotton _____

_____

7. coconuts _____

_____

_____

EXERCISE 2

Use the following words in questions.

1. is _____

2. was _____

3. has _____

4. are _____

5. were _____

6. have _____

EXERCISE 3

Write a command or a request about each of the following things.

1. a horse _____

_____

2. your hat _____

_____

3. a fire _____

_____

4. a door _____

_____

5. your book _____

EXERCISE 4

This dictation exercise focuses on capital letters. On a separate sheet of paper, copy these sentences down as your teacher reads them aloud.

1. Broadway is a main business street in New York.
2. San Francisco has one of the finest harbors in the world.
3. William Penn founded the city of Philadelphia.
4. The first streets were named from trees that grew on that spot.
5. Some of the names were Chestnut, Walnut, Spruce, and Pine.
6. Benjamin Franklin discovered that lightning is a discharge of electricity.
7. Washington Irving wrote the story of Rip Van Winkle.

EXERCISE 5

This dictation exercise focuses on using the comma with direct address. On a separate sheet of paper, copy these sentences down as your teacher reads them aloud.

1. Here, my friends, is a good place for our camp.
2. Mr. Bright, will you join our party?
3. Please, sir, can you tell me the meaning of this riddle?
4. Woodman, spare that tree!
5. Howard, what have you in that box?
6. Listen, my hearers, to this story.
7. "Hush, puppy, hush!" exclaimed the boy
8. Ring, happy bells, across the snow.
9. Stay yet, my friends, a moment stay.

EXERCISE 6

This dictation exercise focuses on using quotation marks. On a separate sheet of paper, copy these sentences down as your teacher reads them aloud.

1. THE BOYS AND THE FROGS
2. One day some boys were playing by a pond.
3. The frogs in the water lifted their heads and cried, "Croak! Croak!"

4. "Oh? Are you there? Then we will stone you!" said the boys.

5. So they began to stone the frogs, when a large frog cried out, "Oh stop! Stop! This is fun for you, but it is death for us."

6. Then the boys saw how cruel they had been and left the frogs in peace.

EXERCISE 7

Write a letter to one of your cousins, telling about something interesting you have done lately. Plan to mail the letter to your cousin.

Summary of Rules

SENTENCES

A **sentence** is the expression of a complete thought in words. (page 1)

Every sentence should begin with a **capital** letter. (page 3)

A **period** (.) should be placed after every complete statement. (page 3)

A **period** (.) should be placed after a command or request. (page 10)

A **question mark** (?) should be placed at the end of a question. (page 6)

A word or sentence that expresses sudden or strong feelings is called an **exclamation**. (page 13)

An exclamation should be followed by an **exclamation point** (!). (page 13)

A series of sentences relating to a particular point or the same subject is called a **paragraph**. (page 17)

NOUNS

Words that tell the names of people, places or things are called **nouns**. (page 20)

Nouns that tell the name of a *specific* person, place or thing are called **proper nouns**. Proper nouns should begin with a **capital** letter. (page 21)

Nouns that *do not* tell the name of *specific* people, places or things are called **common nouns**. Common nouns should begin with a **lowercase** letter. (page 22)

WRITING NAMES AND TITLES

The name that belongs to all the members of the same family is called the **family name**, **last name**, or **surname**. (page 24)

The part of a name given to a child by his parents is called the **given name**, **first name**, or **Christian name**. The given name is sometimes made up of two words. (page 24)

When, instead of a word in a name, you write the initial of that word, use a **capital** letter. (page 26)

Place a **period** (**.**) after each initial. (page 26)

When you write the word *uncle* or the word *aunt* as a part of a name, begin it with a **capital** letter. (page 51)

DAYS, MONTHS, AND SEASONS

The names of the days of the week begin with **capital** letters. (page 35)

The names of the months should begin with **capital** letters. (page 38)

The names of the seasons usually begin with **lowercase** letters. (page 43)

IS AND *ARE*, *WAS* AND *WERE*, AND *HAS* AND *HAVE*

Use the word *is* when speaking of one person or thing.
Use the word *are* when speaking of more than one person or thing. (page 60)

Use *was* when speaking of one.
Use *were* when speaking of more than one. (page 64)

Use *has* in speaking of one.
Use *have* in speaking of more than one. (page 70)

Use the words *have*, *are*, and *were* with the word *you*, whether it refers one or more than one. (page 75)

QUOTATIONS

The little marks (" ") that enclose the exact words used by another person are called **quotation marks**. (page 78)

Every **direct quotation** should be enclosed by **quotation marks**. (page 78)

A **short direct quotation** should be separated from the remainder of the sentence by a **comma** (,). (page 80)

The first word of a **quotation** should begin with a **capital** letter. (page 80)

OTHER

The word *I* should be written with a **capital** letter. (page 29)

A **period** (.) should be placed after an **abbreviation**. (page 40)

The name of the person addressed should be separated from the rest of the sentence by a **comma** (,) or **commas**. (page 83)

An **apostrophe** (') should be used in a contraction wherever one or more letters are left out. (page 86)

11980172R0006

Made in the USA
Lexington, KY
14 November 2011